P9-CPZ-850

The Way I Feel...Sometimes

The Way I Feel... Sometimes

by Beatrice Schenk de Regniers

illustrated by Susan Meddaugh

Clarion Books

TICKNOR & FIELDS: A HOUGHTON MIFFLIN COMPANY

New York

For Francis —B. de R.

For Niko —S. M.

Clarion Books
Ticknor & Fields, a Houghton Mifflin Company
Text copyright © 1988 by Beatrice Schenk de Regniers
Illustrations copyright © 1988 by Susan Meddaugh

All rights reserved. No part of this work may be reproduced
or transmitted in any form or by any means, electronic or
mechanical, including photocopying and recording, or by any
information storage or retrieval system, except as may be
expressly permitted by the 1976 Copyright Act or in writing
by the publisher. Requests for permission should be addressed
in writing to Clarion Books, 52 Vanderbilt Avenue, New York, NY 10017.
Printed in Italy

Library of Congress Cataloging-in-Publication Data
De Regniers, Beatrice Schenk.
 The way I feel—sometimes.

 Summary: Presents a collection of poems about
feelings, from anger to acceptance.
 1. Emotions—Juvenile poetry. 2. Children's
poetry, American. [1. Emotions—Poetry. 2. American
poetry] I. Meddaugh, Susan ill. II. Title.
PS3554.E1155W39 1988   811'.54   87-18245
ISBN 0-89919-647-0

NI 10 9 8 7 6 5 4 3 2 1

Contents

Feeling Mean, Mostly

The Way I *Really* Am

You wouldn't know
to look at me
what a terror I can be.
You think
I'm mousely quiet,
sugar-sweet.
I'm really
stomping on the house,
smashing it to bits
under my feet.

9

Mean Song

*(Read this aloud—or sing it—three times in
a row on days when you wake up feeling MEAN!)*

I'm warning you,
stay out of my way.
Today's my day
for being mean mean mean!
So better stay clear.
Don't even come near
or I'll look at you mean
and you'll *wither away.*

                 Nnnnyah!

Oh, I'm mean mean mean
and I want to be mean.
I want babies to scream
when they see me.
I want dogs to yelp,
cats to climb a tree,
kids to call for help
when they look at me
looking so-o-o mean!

                Mrrrff!

10

So better stay clear.
Keep out of my way.
I got up on the wrong
side of bed today,
and I'm feeling mean—
and I mean *mean*.
Ve-ry MEAN!

Grrrowp!

I feel better already!

Co-op-er-ate

If there's any
word I hate,
it's the word,
co-op-er-ate.

According to the dictionary
(I looked it up and so I'm very
sure)
the word means doing things
together.
But when some grown-up
says to me,
"Co-op-er-ate!"
I know that she (or sometimes he)
means that whether
I like it or not
I'd better do
whatever he (or sometimes she)
wants me to do.

So—

That's why I say
and say again
(I'll say it over, ten-times-ten)
if there is any
word
I hate
it's the word:
co-
op-
er-
ate.

The Churlish Child's Week

(A churlish child is a rude, mean, cross, surly child.)

Mean, mean Monday
Terrible Tuesday
Wormy Wednesday
Thankless Thursday
Fearful Friday
Savage Saturday
Surly Sunday

The Cheerful Child's Week: Marvelous Monday, Terrific Tuesday, Wonderful Wednesday, Thrilling Thursday, Fabulous Friday, Swell Saturday, Super Sunday.

Feeling Better

There Are Days

1.
There are
glad days,
sad days,
mixed-up-good-and-bad days.

2.
There are
days sun-bright,
days a-glow
with love and joy
when I think every
girl and boy
I know
is
great.

3.
And there are
dark days
when I
hate
everyone in sight—
including ME,
including YOU
all my friends
and my relatives, too.

4.
Oh, well…
Oh, *well*…
anyway,
no matter what,
when a day like *that*
is
over,
I can always say,
tomorrow is another day—
Thank goodness!

Brand-New Baby

It sleeps a lot
and cries a lot
and drinks a lot
and pees a lot
and gets a lot of diapers smelly.

That doesn't stop the grown-ups
coming 'round,
adoring.
(Oh, they sound
so silly
and so boring!)

They coo a lot
and moo a lot
and cluck a lot
and squeal a lot:

"Oooh!
Look at its dear little
fingers and toes!
Look at its dear little
feet!
Look at its tiny,
adorable nose!
Oooh!
Isn't it
sweet,
sweet,
sweet!"

Then,
"How does it feel
to have a new baby?"
everyone asks me.
And I think that maybe
I'll tell them the truth:

I feel proud.
I feel glad.
I feel mixed-up-happy-sad.
It isn't all good,
and it isn't all bad.

I wonder if
I should admit
I'm jealous, too—
a little bit.
Would I be misunderstood?

How does it feel?
It's hard to explain.
I don't think I'll try...
Next time they ask me,
I know what I'll say:
I'll sigh a deep sigh
(to show I am bored),
and then I will tell them,
"Oh...it's...OK."

When I Tell You I'm Scared

Sometimes I'm afraid
of imaginary bears.
They're waiting to chase me
up and down the stairs.
I know they're not real.
They're just imaginary.
But all the same,
they're
very
very
scary.

Sometimes I'm afraid
of imaginary creatures
with imaginary claws
and imaginary features.
I know they're not real.
They're just imaginary.
But all the same,
they're
very
very
scary.

Sometimes I see
an imaginary ghost.
That's the kind of thing
that scares me the most.
I know it's not real.
It's just imaginary.
But all the same,
it's
very
VERY

SCARY

So—
when I tell you I'm scared,
please don't say,
"It's just imaginary.
It will go away."
What I want you to say
is, *"Don't worry, dear.*
Nothing can hurt you
so long as I'm here."

Feeling Wishful

I Wish

I wish I had not told my friend
I'd never speak to her again
and please to go away
and stay away
forever.

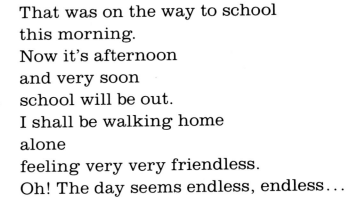

That was on the way to school
this morning.
Now it's afternoon
and very soon
school will be out.
I shall be walking home
alone
feeling very very friendless.
Oh! The day seems endless, endless...

I wish I had not said,
"Drop dead!"
(What if she did! I'd die!)
I think that I
will write a note
right now
to ask her
will she come
to my house
after school today.
And I will say
I'm sorry for what I said,
and tell her how
very bad
I feel.

I think she will
forgive me,
but...
I wish I'd learn to keep my big mouth shut
when I am mad!

What If

What if
my cat
could talk
and give me good advice
(but only when I asked for it)!
Wouldn't that be nice?

What if
my goldfish
learned by heart
forty-five or fifty
lullabies to sing to me!
Wouldn't that be nifty?

What if
my dog
were smart
and taught me how to spell
and helped me with my homework!
Wouldn't that be swell?

What if
my cat,
my dog,
my goldfish
all arranged to meet
and celebrate my birthday!
Wouldn't that be *sweet*?

Queen of the World (or King)

(*If you like, you can substitute* King *for* Queen *as you read this poem.*)

I am Queen of the World today.
Everything has to go my way.
Every *one*
Every *thing*
Must do as I say
      Because I am Queen of the World.

On a windy day,
I wave my hand
And order the wind to
     blow
          blow
              blow.

On a windy day,
At my command
The grasses and the flowers bow
     low
          low
              low.

On a rainy day,
I publish a decree:
Every *one*
Every *thing*
Must listen to me.

Then, looking very grand,
I issue my command:
"Rain, rain!" I say—
And it rains to beat the band
       Because I am Queen of the World.

When the rain is over,
I command it to stop,
And because I am Queen,
Not a single drop
Dares to fall on me
        Because I am Queen of the World.

Oh, it's such a re-spon-si-bil-ity,

It's *such* a responsibility,
I do not often choose to be
        Queen of the World for the day!

Feeling OK, After All

An Important Conversation

Oh.
Hello, Mrs. Jerome.

".......................?"

You want to know
where I'm going
in such a hurry?
I'm running away
from home.

"............?"

No, Mrs. Jerome,
I don't know where—

"...?"

You want to know *why*?
Oh, Mrs. Jerome,
my mother and father,
they're *so* unfair!
They think my little sister
is so cute and sweet.
Everything she does
is just adorable,
they think.
But everything *I* do
is horrible,
they think.

If my little sister cries,
they say to me,
"Stop teasing her!"
All they ever think about
is pleasing her—
Pleasing her
and blaming me
when things go wrong.

So I've decided to run away
and stay away
for a long, long, long
time.
Maybe
until
I'm dead.
And then they'll be sorry.

"......................."

What? Mrs. Jerome?
You said—
You said you heard my mother
say
she was going to make
my favorite dessert today?
But why?

"....................."

Because she wants to do
something special just for me?
My mother said that?
Now Mrs. Jerome,
cross your heart and hope to die?
My mother really said—

"................!"

No, Mrs. Jerome.
Of course I know
you wouldn't lie.
What else did she say?

".........................."

My little sister just *adores* me?
Mrs. Jerome, I'm telling *you*
my little sister *bores* me.
She's just a brat.
She's a big fat zero.
She stinks.

". . . . ."

My father told you
my little sister thinks
that I'm a *hero?*
When did he tell you that?

"...................."

The other day?
Oh, I remember.
I chased a dog away
she thought was going to
get her.
Well,
there are times
when I like my little sister better
than other times.

"............................."

Really?
My father told you
I'll always be his Number One
because I'm his first child
and his only
son?
He said that, hey?

Well, so long now,
Mrs. Jerome.
Nice talking to you,
but I'd better be
getting
home
in time for supper.

DISCARDED

12 PEACHTREE

J811.54

De Regniers, Beatrice Schenk.
   The way I feel ... sometimes / by
Beatrice Schenk de Regniers ;
illustrated by Susan Meddaugh. -- New
York : Clarion Books, c1988.
   48 p. : col. ill. ; 24 cm.
   Summary: Presents a collection of
poems about feelings, from anger to
acceptance.
   ISBN 0-89919-647-0 (lib. bdg.)

R00231 81045

   1. Emotions--Juvenile poetry. 2.
Children's poetry. I. Meddaugh, Susan.
II. Title

DEC 19 1988

GA   11 OCT 88   16226389   GAPApc   87-18245